To Lee, for always supporting my dreams.

For Ella, the best human I know.

First Edition

Library of Congress Control Number: 2023921795

Summary: Esther and Elijah are sent by their mother on a very important errand - to buy a chicken that is sure to impress their very particular grandmother. With money in hand and wagon in tow they set off from their San Francisco home to the neighborhood butcher shop. They request a chicken sure to impress and that's exactly what they receive . . . although it may not be exactly what their mother had in mind.

ISBN 9798-2182-8044-4

Copyright © 2023 by AIMEE LEEB PEARSON

All rights reserved. No part of this book may be reproduced or used in any manner without the prior written permission of the copyright owner, except for the use of brief quotations in a book review.

Inquiries regarding discounts and purchasing can be addressed to Lavender Ink Books.

www.lavenderinkbooks.com

A Chicken Sure to Impress

story by Aimee Pearson
illustrations by Rania Hasan

"Kids," called Mother. "I'm on my way to pick up Grandmother and I need your help. I'd like you to go to the butcher shop and ask for a chicken. You know how particular Grandmother is, so make sure to ask for one that is sure to impress. The butcher will tell you exactly what to do."

Esther and Elijah headed directly to the butcher shop, with their red wagon in tow.

After gathering her courage, Esther stood at the counter, and in a clear and confident voice said, "My mother told us to ask for a chicken sure to impress."

He went to the back room and returned with a large box.

"Now here's what you need to do. First you will wash the chicken. Next, dress the chicken. After that, stuff the chicken. Finally, leave the chicken to cook for two hours."

Elijah said, "Thank you, sir." He handed the butcher their money. It took both children to lift the box into their wagon.

Once home, the children brought the heavy box into the kitchen. Very cautiously, they opened the lid. To their surprise, out popped a fluffy, divinely plump chicken.

She lifted her wings and shook her tail feathers with a swish.
She gave each of the children a sideways chicken glance.

Esther whispered to Elijah, "What do we do now?"

Elijah responded, "Well, the butcher said to wash her first. I guess that's what we should do."

Elijah took a large copper jam pot off a hook on the wall and Esther filled it with soap and water. Before they realized what was happening, the beautiful chicken delicately stepped into the tub.

She rolled around, fluttered her wings, and sent suds sloshing.

After thoroughly making a mess of the kitchen, she hopped out of the tub and gave an elegant shake. Esther and Elijah gave each other a shrug.

Esther said, "I'll get the hair dryer."

The chicken lifted her wings in turn, while the children dried her wet feathers until they were perfectly puffed.

She ran to her room and returned with a basket, overstuffed with dress-up costumes.

Elijah pulled pink airy tutus, flowered hats, and strands of beads out of the basket. Esther began trying items on the chicken. The tutu didn't quite work with her shape, and her small head was lost in a large-brimmed hat. But a strand of pearls looked perfect wrapped twice around her neck.

Esther found a pinafore that added just the right flare. The chicken was beautifully dressed.

Elijah asked, "What should we stuff her with?"

Esther replied, "Well, let's see what we have."

They riffled through the kitchen; then piled celery, onions, garlic, slices of bread, parsley, and various spices into a large mixing bowl. The chicken got right to work. She pecked and scratched and pecked and scratched. Soon she was happily stuffed.

"I guess the only thing left to do now, is leave her to cook," Elijah said.

The children left the kitchen to read and play. From the sitting room, they heard pots clatter and pans sizzle and kettles whistle. They smelled onions frying and vegetables roasting and cakes baking.

Then with a BANG the backdoor slammed.

The children rushed into the kitchen to find Mother and Grandmother in shock at the scene before them. The table was set with Mother's finest linen and silver, and a perfectly cooked family dinner sat waiting. There was even a vase of flowers next to a decorated five-layer cake.

Mother gasped and exclaimed, "Oh dear! There's a chicken in the kitchen!"

Grandmother smiled and said, "Well, I am impressed."

With the chicken at the head of the table, they all sat down to a wonderful meal.

∽ The End ∾

Welcome, young readers. I'm thrilled to introduce you to my book, "A Chicken Sure to Impress." It's a story dear to my heart and a love letter to my family's history in San Francisco.

My grandmother enjoyed a childhood of freedom and adventure in San Francisco. She would often take the cable car for excursions all over the city and, on a whim, hop on the ferry to visit her aunt in Oakland. One of her favorite stories to tell was about the opening day of the Golden Gate Bridge, when she and her sister each paid 25 cents to be among the first to walk across the bay from San Francisco to Marin.

Once she was married, my grandparents settled in the Richmond District on Parker Avenue. Growing up, I listened in wonder as my family shared stories about their beloved Parker Avenue—a place where friends and neighbors were like family, and food was at the center of it all.

My grandmother ran a spotless household with delicious home-cooked meals served for breakfast, lunch, dinner, and of course, dessert. She was so warm and inviting that even today, my mother's friends tell me how my grandmother had the gift of making them feel special when they were growing up. They all wanted her to be their mom, and their moms wanted her recipes!

Now that I'm a mom with my own household, I do my best to honor my grandmother's legacy. Even so, my home is run a bit differently than my grandmother's—it is far from spotless but is filled with lots of laughter and good food. But the biggest difference? Instead of me being in charge, our beloved house chicken rules the roost, even in the kitchen. My grandmother would be horrified if she knew!

Now just imagine what would happen if the perfect mom sent her children to buy the perfect chicken to impress the perfect grandmother with the perfect dinner, but instead, the perfect plan goes askew when the chicken decides to take over the kitchen. That's the inspiration behind "A Chicken Sure to Impress."

I invite you to step into this imaginary misadventure of two children attempting to find a chicken that is sure to impress. Most of all, I hope you enjoy this tribute to my dear grandmother, Carol, who is always with me in spirit.

Thank you for reading.

Aimee Pearson

Printed in the USA
CPSIA information can be obtained
at www.ICGtesting.com
LVHW071123120324
774244LV00004B/99

9 798218 280444